CW00730851

THE PRAYER OF ST THÉRÈSE OF LISIEUX

Vernon Johnson

1938

CATHOLIC TRUTH SOCIETY

PUBLISHERS TO THE HOLY SEE

She shows us that we must pray,
like little children, by love,
in order to obtain love,
"the one thing necessary"…

Mgr Vernon Johnson (1886-1969) was an Anglican clergyman
who became Catholic after visiting the Carmel of Lisieux.

CTS ONEFIFTIES

Originally published as *The Prayer of St Teresa of Lisieux: Part I* and
The Prayer of St Teresa of Lisieux: Part II, 1938. The texts have been
very slightly abridged for this edition.

Published by The Incorporated Catholic Truth Society,
40-46 Harleyford Road London SE11 5AY
www.ctsbooks.org
ISBN 978 1 78469 549 1

THE PRAYER OF ST TERESA OF LISIEUX - PART I

Vernon Johnson

CONTENTS

PART I   PAGE

INTRODUCTION 7

I.   THE NECESSITY OF PRAYER.................................... 9

II.   THE SOURCE OF ST TERESA'S PRAYER 12

III.   THE CHARACTER OF ST TERESA'S PRAYER—

       Its Love 14
       Its Humility..... 17
       Its Confidence.. 19
       Its Abandonment...................................... 22
       Its Simplicity 25

IV.   THE HOLY EUCHARIST AND THE PRAYER OF ST TERESA 29

The author wishes to express his deep gratitude to the Carmelites of Lisieux without whose supervision and encouragement this little book would never have been written.

In the chapter on "Dryness in Prayer" the author wishes to express his indebtedness to *The Science of Prayer* by Ludovic de Besse, O.S.F.C.

REFERENCES

A.—Autobiography; L.—Laveille; N.V.—Novissima Verba; S.—Spirit of St Teresa.

THE PRAYER OF ST TERESA

St Teresa of The Child Jesus, commonly known as the Little Flower, was raised up by Almighty God to teach us the Little Way of Spiritual Childhood.

In it she teaches us to look upon God always as Our Father, and ourselves as His little children; to treat Him with that love and humility, confidence and abandonment, which marks the relationship of any little child with its parent. It was in order that she might teach us this Little Way that she was canonized by the Holy See.

But the Little Way of Spiritual Childhood is not the fruit of our own unaided human effort. It is the result of the co-operation of our will with the grace of God. This grace, without which we can neither understand nor follow the Little Way, we can only obtain by prayer.

And so our generation turns to St Teresa, the teacher of the Little Way of Spiritual Childhood, the messenger of Jesus, as long ago the Apostles turned to their Master Himself, saying: "Teach us to pray."[1] She answers our appeal by the beautiful teaching of her life and of her writings. She tells us of the necessity of prayer. She shows us that the foundation of all prayer lies in belief in the Fatherhood of God, "the Father of lights, from whom comes every good and perfect gift."[2] She shows us that we must pray, like little children, by love, in order to obtain love, "the one thing necessary," and that we must pray with humility and confidence, with a complete abandonment to the Divine Will, and with utter simplicity. She teaches us how to pray, not only in moments of consolation, but also in the midst of dryness and, above

---

[1] Luke xi. 1.
[2] James i. 17.

all, in the hour of suffering and spiritual desolation. Finally, she teaches us, and this is the main point in her teaching, that in truth there is only one Prayer—the Prayer of Jesus, the Sacrifice of Calvary, continued in our midst to-day upon the altars of the Church—and that it is from this prayer, and from this prayer alone, that all other prayers derive their reality and power.

THE NECESSITY OF PRAYER

"It is by prayer and sacrifice alone that we Carmelites can be useful to the Church."[1] These words are the key to the life of St Teresa and to the life of every Carmelite nun. She gave herself to God in a life of prayer and sacrifice, in order that, being entirely given to God, she might, therefore, be entirely given to the work of the salvation of souls. She did not enter Carmel in order to escape from the world, but just in order that she might be in the very heart of the world and might help souls in the fullest possible way.

On her journey to Rome, when she was not yet fifteen, a fellow pilgrim handed her the Annals of some Missionary Sisters. After accepting them eagerly, she passed them on to her sister, saying to her: "I will not read them, for I find I am too anxious for active works, and I wish to be hidden in a cloister so as to give myself more completely to God."[2] She means by that, to sacrifice all the consolation and satisfaction of an active apostolate, in order to give herself to the greatest apostolate of all, a life of prayer and sacrifice. In her eyes prayer was the vital foundation of all activity. "The power of prayer," she says, "has been understood by all the Saints, and especially, perhaps, by those who have illumined the world with the light of Christ's teaching. Was it not from prayer that St Paul, St Augustine, St Thomas Aquinas, St John of the Cross, St Teresa, and so many other friends of God, acquired the wonderful knowledge which has enthralled the loftiest minds? The Almighty gave them the prayer that inflames with the fire of love. Thus they have uplifted the world—thus do the Saints who

---

[1] N.V., p. 56.
[2] L., p. 137.

still combat on earth raise it to-day, and will continue to raise it, till the end of time."[1]

It is so easy to be captivated by the external activities of a life and to forget the prayer that must lie behind them if these activities are to have any supernatural value at all. It is easy to be caught by the glamour of St Teresa and not to realize the prayer which is the source of all her power.

It is so, even in the Life of Our Blessed Lord. We all know that He chose twelve Apostles; we all know that He gave us the Lord's Prayer; we all know that He was transfigured on Mount Tabor. But how many of us realize that Our Lord prepared for each of these occasions by going aside to pray? "And it came to pass in those days, that he went out into a mountain to pray, and he passed the whole night in the prayer of God."[2] Thus did He prepare for choosing the Apostles. It was the same when He gave us the Lord's Prayer: "And it came to pass, that as he was in a certain place praying, when he ceased, one of his disciples said to him: Lord, teach us to pray…. And he said to them: When you pray, say: Father…"[3] And on Mount Tabor, at the Transfiguration, we are told: "And whilst he prayed, the shape of his countenance was altered, and his raiment became white and glittering."[4] It was by an agony of prayer in Gethsemane that He prepared for His approaching Passion. And these were but specially noted occasions of what was, with Our Blessed Lord, a continual habit of prayer. St Mark tells us so: "And rising very early, going out, he went into a desert place: and there he prayed."[5] Here we have a glimpse of that continual background of prayer which was the source of Our Lord's Public Ministry. Above all, these were but the prelude to the one perfect prayer which Our Lord offered to the Father when He gave Himself for us upon the Cross. The Sacrifice of Calvary is a living prayer, the one and only perfect prayer,

---

[1] A., p. 194.
[2] Luke vi. 12.
[3] Luke xi. 1.
[4] Luke ix. 29.
[5] Mark i. 35.

which alone can save the world. All other prayers derive their power from the Cross. The self-oblation of contemplative souls, whose life is a perpetual prayer, owes its particular power to the fact that it is such an intimate sharing in the Self-Oblation of Our Lord on Calvary. The Holy Father himself has no doubt about this particular prayer, and he is anxious that we should fully realize it. "Contemplatives contribute a great part to the progress of the Church and to the salvation of the human race, far more than those who work in the harvest of the Lord. For if the former did not call down from Heaven an abundant rain of Divine graces to make this harvest fertile, the workers of the Gospel would reap less fruit."[1]

Our Lord made prayer the background of His Life, and what He did Himself He teaches us to do as well. "And he spoke also a parable to them, that we ought always to pray, and not to faint."[2] "Faint"—that is just the word. It is not that we disbelieve in prayer; but we just lose heart and collapse from prayer into mere activity, and our works lose all their supernatural savour. In this rushing materialistic age we need a simple guide to lead us back to prayer. Almighty God has answered our need. In so doing, He has chosen neither a learned theologian nor a master of oratory, but a simple nun, hidden in a convent. He stripped her of every activity except that of prayer and sacrifice, and, in a shortness of time quite unparalleled, He has made her loved by all the world. Why? Just to teach us the vital importance, the absolute necessity, of prayer. Most people know of the roses let fall upon the earth by St Teresa; some know and love her Little Way, but few even of those know much about her prayer. And yet her prayer was her supreme activity when she was on the earth, and it is the secret of her power to-day. "In prayer and sacrifice lies all my strength. Experience has taught me that they touch hearts far more easily than words."[3]

---

[1] Extract from the Apostolic Constitutions approving the Institution of the Order of Chartreux, July 9th, 1924.
[2] Luke xviii. 1.
[3] A., p. 179.

THE SOURCE OF
ST TERESA'S PRAYER

The Fatherhood of God

One day a Sister entered St Teresa's cell and found her sewing. As she entered, the Sister noticed a wonderful expression on the face of the Saint. "What are you thinking of?" the Sister asked.

St Teresa replied: "I was meditating on the 'Our Father.' It is so wonderful to be able to call God, Our Father."[1] As she said this, her eyes filled with tears. To the superficial critic this scene may seem emotional and sentimental, whereas, really, in its simplicity, it is profound. For in it we have the source of the whole of the prayer of St Teresa. It all flows from the Fatherhood of God. It takes a saint to be simple enough to see so vividly and profoundly all the truth contained in the two words, "Our Father," that she could not get beyond them without her eyes filling with tears. It is just because we are so complex and so superficial that we cannot get to the heart of things. We repeat the words, "Our Father," over and over again, and never realize the wonders which these two words contain. The truth is that the Saint, in her simplicity, is at the very heart of Scripture. When the disciples asked Our Lord: "Lord, teach us to pray," it is these two words which Our Lord, in His Divine Love and Wisdom, places upon their lips: "Thus therefore you shall pray: Our Father."[2] To St Teresa, as she meditated on it, this scene of Scripture was overwhelming. These words, "Our Father," were spoken by Him who Himself was God made Man, the supreme revelation on

---

[1] A., p. 213.
[2] Matt. vi. 9.

earth of that very Father of whom He was speaking. In Him she saw and heard the Father. Her whole soul went out in complete response to this amazing revelation that God was her Father and she was His child, and that all those around her were just His children, too. This simple truth, in all its fullness, is hidden from the wise and prudent and revealed to little ones.[1] St Teresa saw this truth in all its beauty, just because she looked upon her Heavenly Father with the eyes of a little child. It is to call us back to this simplicity in our prayer that God has given her to us to-day.

Not merely is St Teresa at the heart of Scripture, but she is at the heart of theology as well. That we might be able to say once again "Our Father," not merely with our lips, but with that complete response of a life in which the will is entirely surrendered to that Father's Love— this was the whole object of our Redemption. St Paul tells us that this is the supreme work of the Holy Trinity in our soul. "Because ye are sons God hath sent the spirit of his Son into your hearts, crying Abba, Father."[2] The Father's plan was, through the Holy Spirit, to re-establish all things in Christ, to give us back the power to say, with our whole being, "Our Father," a thing we had been unable to do ever since the Fall, and so to restore to us all that, through the Fall, we had lost— sanctifying grace, a life of supernatural love, a sharing in the Godhead, a place in the family of Our Father, to become again the children of God—all this is exquisitely focused to a point in these two precious words, "Our Father." They constitute indeed Heaven on earth, for that is what the life of grace is. Listen again to St Teresa:

"To call God my Father and to know myself His child, That, that is Heaven to me."

(*Poem* "My Heaven.")

Accurate theology in the simple language of the Saint.

---

[1] Matt. xi. 25.
[2] Galatians iv. 6.

THE CHARACTER OF THE PRAYER
OF ST TERESA

Its Love

To St Teresa, meditating simply and frequently on the two words, "Our Father," prayer became at once an expression of love.

It could not be otherwise. For these two words told her that God was her Father and she His little child. In ordinary human life, the relationship of the little child to its father is above all, a relationship of love. The little child is always endeavouring to express its love in order to receive more love from the parent. In the same way, the parent is always expressing his love so as to receive the love of the little child. Both love in order to be loved. It is, as it were, a duet, each striving by their love to draw forth more love from the other.

The prayer of St Teresa is the prayer of a little child to its father. The supreme object in St Teresa's prayer was to console the Heart of her Heavenly Father by giving Him the love which He had created her to give Him, and for which He thirsts; and also to satisfy the craving of her soul by calling down into her heart the Divine Love for which she was made. All through her life this desire to love and be loved is found expressed in her prayer. "Jesus, I ask for love, boundless, limitless love. One thought is mine, dear Jesus, it is to love Thee."[1] "O my God, I know it, love is repaid by love alone." Her object is always to console her Heavenly Father by giving Him the love for which He thirsted, and, in so doing, to draw down into her soul the Divine Love for which she craved.

But the words, "Our Father," meant more to her than this. They filled her with longing that this might be true of all the other children of her Heavenly Father. And so she gathers them all into her prayer. "I wish, O my God, to work for Thy Love alone, and to save souls who will

---

[1] A., p. 136.

love Thee for ever."[1] Thus her vision widens, and her prayer becomes a craving that all the family may love their Heavenly Father and so console His Heart and, at the same time, draw down upon them the love for which they were made and without which they will never be at rest. All humanity comes within the orbit of her prayer. To win back the world to that Father's Love, which she saw on all sides being rejected, so as to console that Father's Heart, that is the second object of her prayer.

It was with this twofold object that St Teresa made her Act of Oblation. On June 9th, 1895, the feast of the Holy Trinity, she definitely offered herself as victim to the merciful Love of God, to console her Heavenly Father's Heart for the souls which rejected Him, and to win back those souls to His love.

This Act of Oblation was written out by her and signed with her own hand. In it we find the essence of her prayer. We can only quote a few words—"O my God, O Most Blessed Trinity, I desire to love Thee and to make Thee loved—I wish to labour for Thy love alone, with the sole aim of pleasing Thee, of consoling Thy Sacred Heart and of saving souls who will love Thee through all Eternity—In order that my life may be one act of perfect love I offer myself as a victim to Thy merciful love."[2]

Reading this, we are tempted to say—this is all very well for perfect souls—but it is not for me! This is wrong. St Teresa herself tells us that *all* souls of good will who follow her Little Way can make their offering. Writing to her sister, she says: "Dear Sister, you who love Jesus and long to be His little victim, do you not understand that the more weak and wretched we are the better material do we make for His consuming and transfiguring fire? The simple desire to be a victim suffices; but we must also consent to remain always poor and helpless."[3]

There is nothing fanciful or high-flown in this. It is simple Scripture. "He was in the world, and the world was made by him, and the world knew him not. He came unto his own and his own received him not:

---

[1] Act of Oblation, A., p. 448.
[2] A., p. 447.
[3] A., p. 360.

but as many as received him, he gave them power to become the sons of God."[1] To console her Heavenly Father's Heart for this rejection she would offer her life as an act of perfect love. It is all so simple and yet so deep. Its simplicity attracts us, its depth alarms us. But it is wrong to be afraid. For what is this prayer but the expression of that life of supernatural love, the Very Life of God for which we were made, and which is involved in the two words, "Our Father"? We need not fear. For this life of love does not depend primarily on us. It is the work of the Holy Trinity dwelling within us, placed in our souls at Baptism by our holy Mother the Church.

This gift of supernatural love is the special work of the Holy Spirit. "The charity of God is poured forth in our hearts by the Holy Ghost who is given to us."[2] It is, first of all, God's Gift. To this Gift of the Holy Spirit within us, it is our life's work to respond. St Teresa saw this clearly. And so it is to the Holy Trinity to whom she offers her great prayer of self-oblation. "O my God, O Most Blessed Trinity, I desire to love Thee and to make Thee loved."[3]

Finally, this life of supernatural love is the beginning, here and now, of our life in Heaven.

"My Heaven, I have found it in the Holy Trinity, Which dwells
    within my heart,
The Prisoner of my love."

(*Poem* "To live by Love.")

For Heaven is the Life of the Holy Trinity in all its fullness, a life of limitless, unhindered, changeless love. Heaven for us in the future depends upon our response here and now to the Holy Trinity dwelling within us as the result of our Baptism. St Teresa tells us so: "In Heaven there is a place kept for us: if we but love Jesus truly together with Our Father in the spirit of Love."[4]

---

[1] John i. 10.
[2] Rom. v. 5.
[3] A., p. 447.
[4] A., p. 3o8.

Its Humility

A little child depends entirely upon its father. It depends upon its father's love for everything. Yet the father loves the little child to tell him its desires and requests; and the more it asks the happier the father is, for it is his delight to give generously in response. But, though the little child makes its own little efforts, it depends really entirely upon the father. It is the same with the prayer of St Teresa. Her prayer was essentially one of complete dependence on her Father's Love. She realized that she owed all her prayer to the fact that her Father had given her the power to pray and desired to hear her making her requests. So her prayer was always an expression of deep humility. "The moment," she says, "that God sees we are convinced of our nothingness He stretches out His Hand."[1] This is the essential spirit of the prayer of the Little Way of Spiritual Childhood. In another place she says: "God gives generously, but He will have humility of heart."[2] Here again she is but echoing Holy Scripture: "God giveth grace to the humble."[3]

To realize our nothingness apart from God is one of the most difficult things in the world. One of the great results of sin and of the Fall has been to blind us so that we think we are independent of God. We become self-confident and independent, seeking self-love all the time, and trying to twist God's Will to ours. This is especially obvious in our prayers. We think we know what to pray for, how to pray for it, and exactly when and how the answer to our prayer should come. The prayer of the Apostles, James and John, is a perfect example of this wrong kind of prayer: "Master, we desire that whatsoever we shall ask, thou wouldst do it for us."[4] We forget that we are sinners, blinded by the Fall. It needs a real conversion if we are to become like little children in our prayers. "Little children do not know what is good for them,"[5] so St Teresa loved to say. Their prayer must, therefore, be very

---

[1] A., p. 303.
[2] A., p. 347.
[3] James iv. 6.
[4] Mark x. 35.
[5] A., p. 294.

humble. It must always be: "Father, not what I will, but what Thou wilt."[1]

One of her favourite parables was that of the Pharisee and the Publican, just because the prayer of the Publican so exactly expressed the prayer of the Little Way. "I leave the Pharisee to go his way," she said, "while I repeat with confidence the prayer of the Publican, 'God, be merciful to me, a sinner.'"[2]

She kept this spirit in her prayer to the very end. A few weeks before her death, she said: "When I said the Confiteor before Communion this morning, I felt myself to be, like the Publican, 'a great sinner.'"[3] It is only this sense of our own sinfulness and, therefore, of our own inability to know what to pray for as we ought that keeps us, in our prayer, safe from that fatal danger of thinking that we can judge as to what we ought to pray for, and as to when and how the answer to our prayer should come. There is nothing exaggerated in this attitude of humility and dependence in our prayer, because humility is seeing the truth and accepting it. And the truth is that God is everything, and that, without Him, we are nothing. Without this attitude, our prayer is imperfect in its love, both towards our Heavenly Father and those around us.

For this humility Teresa was ever praying, because she knew that humility alone would set her free to love her Father and those around her as she desired. "Dear Jesus," she says, "I implore Thee to send me a humiliation whenever I desire to set myself above others. Thou knowest my weakness."[4] "O Jesus, when Thou wast on this earth Thou didst say: 'Learn of me, for I am meek and humble of heart, and you shall find rest to your souls.'"[5] "I understand, dear Lord, these words which come from Thy meek and humble Heart, and I desire to put

---

[1] Mark xiv. 36.
[2] A., p. 194.
[3] N.V., 137.
[4] N.V., p. 202.
[5] Matt. xi. 29.

them in practice with the help of Thy grace. I desire to humble myself in all sincerity."[1]

The humility of St Teresa is so devastating that we are tempted to think that it is impossible for us. But that would be to miss the whole point of her Little Way. For the source from which this humility sprang was not her own unaided efforts. It sprang from the life of the Holy Trinity within her. Self-love may blind us so that often we may not pray aright, but we are not left alone. To say the words, "Our Father," in all their fullness does indeed require a deep humility; but to enable us to say these words is the express work of the Holy Spirit. Scripture tells us plainly that the Holy Spirit will give us all the aid we need. "The Spirit also helpeth our infirmities. For we know not what we can pray for as we ought: but the Spirit himself asketh for us."[2]

The consciousness that, if her prayer was to be in any way an expression of her love, it must be based upon humility, is beautifully expressed in a prayer which she wrote on a picture in her breviary: "Lord, Thou knowest that I love Thee; but have pity on me, because I am only a sinner."[3] Both these prayers she takes from the Gospels, and it is upon the Gospels that she bases what is perhaps the most beautiful of all her prayers for humility: "O my God, Thou canst do all things, deign to implant in my soul the humility which I desire, and to obtain it from Thine infinite Mercy I will often say: 'Jesus, meek and humble of heart, make my heart like unto Thine.'"[4]

Its Confidence

In ordinary human life, out of the loving dependence of a little child springs a complete confidence in its father. It never occurs to a little child that its father could fail it. It is the same with the prayer of St Teresa. To her the two words, "Our Father," spelt confidence. Her

[1] A., pp. 453 and 454.
[2] Rom. viii. 26.
[3] John xxi. 16; Luke, xviii. 13.
[4] A., p. 454.

confidence knew no bounds. The Father who had made her to love Him, and upon whom she so utterly depended, could not fail to answer the prayers of a child who loved Him, provided they were made with deep humility and a really surrendered will. To her this was just sheer logic. So, from her sense of a complete dependence, there sprang not a morbid consciousness of her weakness, but an audacity which knew no limits. "From the good God we obtain all that we hope for,"[1] she was constantly saying. As her excuse for her audacity she quotes the simple fact that she is her Father's little child: "O my God, I dare not try to understand all that my prayer means. I should fear to be crushed by the mere weight of its audacity. That I am Thy child is my only excuse, for children do not grasp the full meaning of their words. Yet if their parents were to mount a throne and inherit vast wealth, they would not hesitate to grant the desires of their little ones, who are dearer to them than life itself. To please them they would spend most lavishly, stooping even to weakness."[2]

Once again it is not mere fancy. For Our Blessed Lord has revealed exactly this in the story of the Prodigal Son. When the elder son complained because the father was lavishing upon the prodigal special manifestations of his love, the father replied: "Son, thou art always with me and all that I have is thine."[3] St Teresa revelled in these last words, for they revealed so completely the generosity of the Father in Heaven to those who tread the Little Way. Those who tread the Little Way of Spiritual Childhood, the way of loving dependence and complete confidence in their Father's Love, can never stray far from that Love, and therefore are always with Him. They need no special manifestations of that Father's Love, for all that He has is theirs. St Teresa saw this with the simple vision of a little child, and, seeing it thus, she knew there was simply no limit to what the Father would give her. All that He had was really and truly hers. Therefore, she knew that

---

[1] L., p. 309.
[2] A., p. 205.
[3] Luke xv. 31.

her prayers would always be answered. This confidence was absolute, without any wavering, and was not based on any fleeting emotion, but upon the explicit promise of Our Lord Himself. "During the days of His Life on earth Thy Divine Son, my Sweet Spouse, spoke these words: 'If you ask the Father anything in My name He will give it you.' Therefore I am certain Thou wilt grant my prayer."[1]

Again and again Our Lord, in the Gospels, seeks to give us this confidence. "All things whatsoever you shall ask in prayer, believing, you shall receive."[2] "And I say to you, Ask, and it shall be given you, seek, and you shall find, knock, and it shall be opened to you. For everyone that asketh, receiveth; and he that seeketh, findeth; and to him that knocketh, it shall be opened."[3] This Our Blessed Lord promises in the Gospels, and then He gives the ground of our confidence that His promises are true. "And which of you, if he ask his father bread, will he give him a stone? or a fish, will he for a fish give him a serpent? or, if he shall ask an egg, will he give him a scorpion? If you then, being evil, know how to give good gifts to your children, how much more will your Father from heaven give the good spirit to them that ask him?"[4] In other words, if a human father's heart is loving and generous, how much more the Heart of Our Father who is in Heaven. St Teresa's confidence did not rest in whether her prayers seemed to be answered or no, but simply in the word of Our Blessed Lord. In the midst of complete darkness this confidence never wavered, because she did not trust merely in what she felt or saw or understood, but solely in the promise of Our Lord Jesus Christ.

It is this confidence which St Teresa would teach us; and it is just this confidence which we all need so badly. We all hesitate and fear and waver in the matter of our prayers, precisely because we are so influenced by our own ideas as to how and when and where our prayers should be answered; and when our ideas are not fulfilled we

---

[1] A., p. 447.
[2] Matt. xxi. 22.
[3] Luke xi. 10.
[4] Luke xi. 11.

get distressed. To have complete confidence, as St Teresa had, we must place our trust where she placed hers, that is, in the promises of Jesus Christ Himself. This confidence may seem beyond us, a confidence which trusts entirely to the generosity of the Father's Heart, but it is an essential part of the Little Way of Spiritual Childhood. For our comfort, let us remember once again that St Teresa did not arrive at this confidence through her merely human efforts. It was the work of the Holy Trinity within her, to which she responded with such simple faith. This confidence is the special gift of the Holy Spirit. "For you have not received the spirit of bondage again in fear, but you have received the spirit of adoption of sons, whereby we cry: Abba, Father."[1]

To the Holy Spirit, then, we must turn if we would possess the confidence of the child of God.

"O my God, I am certain Thou wilt answer my prayer. I know that the more Thou wishest to bestow, the more Thou makest us to desire. In my heart I feel boundless desire. I confidently beseech Thee to take possession of my soul."[2]

Its Abandonment

Closely allied to humility and confidence in a little child is the spirit of "abandon" which we find in little children. We must be careful to remember that in English we have no word which exactly expresses what we are now trying to consider. In English, the word "abandonment" has a note of despair, whereas the "abandon" of which St Teresa speaks in her Little Way is exactly the opposite of despair. It is, on the contrary, the little child flinging itself into its parent's arms with a radiant confidence that all is well, and resting at peace in the certainty that no harm can come to it.

Some may think that this Abandonment is the supreme result of the Little Way of Spiritual Childhood, achieved only by those who reach

[1] Rom. viii. 15.
[2] A., p. 447.

the great spiritual heights. In its perfection, no doubt, this may be true. But it is equally true that, in St Teresa's eyes, it is a characteristic of the Little Way from the very beginning. "Jesus," she says, "was pleased to show me that the only path which leads to the Divine Love is the abandonment of a little child who sleeps without fear in its father's arms."[1] It will be found, then, at the outset, in those who follow the Little Way. It was so in the life of St Teresa, even before she entered Carmel. After the failure of her appeal to the Holy Father during the pilgrimage to Rome, she writes: "For some time past I had offered myself to the Child Jesus to be His little ball. I told Him to treat me just as it might please Him. In a word, I desired to amuse the Holy Child, to give myself up to all His childish fancies…. You can imagine, dear Mother, the desolation of this little ball as it lay neglected on the ground. Yet it continued to hope against hope."[2]

Throughout her life in Carmel St Teresa never ceased to practise this complete abandonment in all her prayer to her Heavenly Father. "I have never," she writes, "sought to ask favours of the Good God. If, for instance, I had said on the day of my First Communion: 'My God, grant me the favour of dying young,' I should regret it very greatly to-day, because I should not be sure of having done His Will alone."[3]

Referring to the day of her Profession, rather more than a year after her entry to Carmel, she tells us: "I was told to beg for the recovery of our darling father; but I was unable to make any other prayer than this: 'O my God, I beseech Thee that it may be Thy Will for Papa to recover.'"[4]

"From my childhood," she tells us, "those words of Job's delighted me: 'Though he kill me, yet will I trust in Him.' I admit that it has taken a long time to arrive at this degree of self-abandonment; but I have reached it now, and it is Our Lord Himself who has brought me there."[5]

---

[1] A., p. 197.
[2] A., p. 115.
[3] S., p. 141.
[4] S., p. 143.
[5] A., p. 222.

Here we see the foundation of her abandonment—Our Blessed Lord Himself. It did not lie in her natural courage, but in her simple faith in Our Lord's own words. "It is the Gospel above all that is the source of my prayer. From it I draw all that is needful for my little soul."[1]

In the Gospels she heard Our Blessed Lord assuring her that her Heavenly Father loved her, and was directing all the events of her life for her highest good. "Your Father knoweth what is needful for you before you ask him."[2] Again: "If you ask the Father anything in my name he will give it you…. And I say not that I will ask the Father for you, for the Father himself loveth you."[3] It was on this revelation—that God was her All-Knowing and All-Loving Father—that she staked her trust. In all her greatest trials this spirit of abandonment to the Divine Will never left her. "At the moment of my greatest trials, when it was my turn to intone the psalms in the choir, if you only knew with what abandonment I would say out loud the verse: 'In Thee, O Lord, have I hoped.'"[4] Never would she allow her prayer to become a cry of despair. Here again, it is to Holy Scripture that she goes for her inspiration. This time it is the storm at sea. "Behold a great tempest arose in the sea, so that the boat was covered with waves, but Jesus was asleep. And the disciples came to him, and awaked him, saying: Lord, save us, we perish. And Jesus saith to them: Why are you fearful, O ye of little faith? Then rising up he commanded the winds, and the sea, and there came a great calm."[5] Speaking of one of her retreats, she says: "I was seemingly abandoned by God. Jesus slept in my boat, as was His wont. But how rarely will souls allow Him to sleep in peace! In all probability He will sleep on till my great and everlasting retreat; this, however, rather rejoices than grieves me."[6]

This simple abandonment to the Will of God, when God seems asleep, in our prayer is possible for all whose prayer is based on the

---

[1] S., p. 165.
[2] Matt. vi. 8.
[3] John xvi. 23, 26, 27.
[4] S., p. 143.
[5] Matt. viii. 24.
[6] A., p. 134.

love, humility, and confidence of the Little Way, provided we place all our hope, not in anything that we feel, nor in the understanding of the plan that God is working out for us, but simply and solely in the certain truth, as it comes from the lips of Our Blessed Lord—that God is Our Heavenly Father, all-powerful, all-knowing, all-loving. This certainty, if we will only be simple enough to surrender ourselves to it, will set our souls free from all that anxious worry, all that fear and lack of confidence which makes our prayers so uncertain, so weak, so feeble. "We know," says St Paul, "that for them that love God all things work together unto good."[1] The difference between St Teresa and ourselves is just this: that she saw this truth with the eyes of a child, and with the simplicity of a little child was able to make the spontaneous, unquestioning response which only a little child can make—the response of the complete abandonment of the little child who surrenders itself with unquestioning confidence into its father's arms. "Whosoever shall not receive the kingdom of God as a little child, shall not enter into it."[2]

Its Simplicity

The prayer of St Teresa is the prayer of a little child who knows that it is loved by its father and who, therefore, seeks to love him in return. It is, therefore, simple and not complicated. She prays with the simplicity of a little child. This simplicity is one of its most attractive characteristics. When little children wish to speak to their parents, they do so in the simplest words. Nor do they make long speeches in order that their desires may be known. It is exactly the same with those who follow the Little Way of Spiritual Childhood. They do not make long prayers. Nor do they use complicated or complex forms. St Teresa's prayer was simplicity itself. "The power of prayer is indeed wonderful," she says…. "To secure a hearing there is no need to recite

---

[1] Rom. viii. 28.
[2] Mark x. 15.

set prayers composed for the occasion—were this the case I should indeed deserve to be pitied! Apart from the Divine Office, which, in spite of my unworthiness, is a daily joy, I have not the courage to search through books for beautiful prayers; they are so numerous that it would only make my head ache, and besides, each one is more lovely than the other. Unable either to say them all, or to choose between them, I do as a child would who cannot read—I say just what I want to say to God quite simply, and He never fails to understand."[1]

It would be difficult to find words more human and yet more supernatural. They are full of the simple confidence of a little child. "He never fails to understand." She just opens her heart, and her Heavenly Father always understands. How did she know this? Because she felt it? Not necessarily so, for she prayed, for the most part, in the dark. Feelings are a very uncertain guide in prayer. How, then, did she know it? Her very words: "He never fails to understand," give us the clue. For they are but an echo of Our Blessed Lord's own words: "Your Father knoweth that you have need of all these things."[2] She bases her confidence, not on any feelings of her own, but on the assurances of Our Blessed Lord, in the very words of Christ Himself revealing. "For me," she says, "prayer is an uplifting of the heart, a glance towards Heaven, a cry of gratitude and of love in times of sorrow as well as of joy."[3] So many of us become discouraged with our prayers, because we regard them as something long and wearying. We never realize that prayer is essentially simple. It is just saying the two words, "Our Father," as a little child, just a simple lifting up of the heart, a thought raised towards God, a glance towards Him, a little word of gratitude, not only when things seem to go well, but when they seem to go badly, too. We are only little children who do not know what is good for us. But we do know that Our Heavenly Father loves us, and always gives us what is best.

We find the same simplicity in her prayer for others. "The days would be too short to ask in detail for the needs of each soul, and I am

---

[1] A., p. 179.
[2] Matt. vi. 32.
[3] A., p. 180.

afraid I might forget something important. Complicated methods are not for simple souls, and as I am one of these, Our Lord Himself has inspired me with a very simple way of fulfilling my obligations. One day, after Holy Communion, He made me understand these words of Solomon: 'Draw me, we will run after Thee to the odour of Thy ointments.' O my Jesus, there is then no need to say: In drawing me, draw also the souls that I love. The words, 'Draw me,' suffice. When a soul has been captivated by the odour of Thy perfumes she cannot run alone; as a natural consequence of her attraction towards Thee, all those whom she loves are drawn in her train. As a torrent bears down to the depths of the sea whatever it meets on its way, so likewise, my Jesus, does the soul that plunges into the boundless ocean of Thy Love bring with it all its treasures! My treasures, as Thou well knowest, are the souls which it has pleased Thee to unite with mine, and which Thou Thyself hast confided to me…I ask Jesus to draw me into the fire of His Love, and to unite me so closely to Himself that He may live and act in me. I feel that the more the fire of love consumes my heart, the more frequently shall I cry: 'Draw me!' and the more also will those souls who come in contact with mine 'ran swiftly in the sweet odour of the Beloved.'"[1]

"Draw me." Such simple prayers as this we can offer at any moment of the day, even in the midst of our busiest occupations. Here again we see how perfectly the Little Way of Spiritual Childhood is adapted to the age in which we live, with all its busy rush and its complex and wearying routine. The prayer of St Teresa becomes possible to us whether we pray for the Glory of God, for our own souls, or for the souls of those around us. All we need to do is to glance towards Our Heavenly Father and tell Him all in the very simplest way. Holy Scripture is full of such prayers. "Lord, all my desire is before Thee."[2] Could any prayer better express the longings of the childlike soul in the presence of its Father?

---

[1] A., pp. 190, 191, 193.
[2] Ps. xxxvii. 9.

This simple method of prayer runs throughout the whole of the Gospels, for the prayers that were offered to Our Blessed Lord when He was on the earth were exactly such: "Lord, increase our faith, he whom thou lovest is sick."

Such simplicity in prayer is one of the things we need to learn the most. To call us back to such simplicity is one of the reasons why Our Heavenly Father has given St Teresa to His Church to-day.

THE HOLY EUCHARIST AND THE
PRAYER OF ST TERESA

As we read of the prayer of St Teresa we are filled with a sense of our helplessness. We feel that we can never arrive at such heights as she did. Never can we respond to the Love of Our Heavenly Father in such a way as to be completely consumed by His merciful Love. To become thus a victim to His Love is beyond our power. In other words, we cannot be little enough to surrender ourselves as little children into His arms, which, St Teresa tells us, is the only way to perfection.

We are wrong. We forget that we possess the same source as she from which to draw for our strength. That source is the Mass. The Mass is the Sacrifice of Our Lord Jesus Christ on the Cross, inasmuch as it is the continuation, the renewal, of that Sacrifice in the Church to-day.

All salvation, all grace, flow from the Cross. St Teresa tells us how vividly this was brought home to her one morning at Mass, when she was only fourteen and a half. "One Sunday, on closing my book at the end of Mass, the picture of the Crucifixion slipped partly out, showing one of the Divine Hands pierced and bleeding. My heart was grieved at the sight of the Precious Blood falling to the ground with no one caring to treasure it as it fell. At once I resolved to remain continually in spirit at the foot of the Cross, that I might receive the Divine dew of salvation, and pour it forth on souls. From that day the cry of my Dying Saviour, 'I thirst,' has echoed insistently in my heart, kindling within it new fires of zeal. To give my Beloved to drink was my constant desire. I was consumed with an insatiable thirst for souls."[1] We see her taking

---

[1] A., p. 88.

her stand with unerring instinct at the foot of the Cross, the source of all grace.

But, since the Mass is the Sacrifice of the Cross, the Mass is, therefore, the one sufficient prayer. No prayer can be added to it; all prayer is derived from it. The Mass is the perfect prayer of Christ and His Mystical Body, to which He is united as Head. It is, therefore, the prayer of all the members of the Mystical Body, the prayer of all the children of God. It will then be full of the spirit of the Little Way of Spiritual Childhood, for it will be the prayer of little children to their Heavenly Father. It will be a prayer possessing a vivid sense of the Divine Fatherhood and of the love, humility, confidence, abandon, and simplicity of little children. St Teresa's devotion to the Mass was very great. We see her as a tiny child running out in torrents of rain so as not to miss her Sunday Mass. Later on she begged to be allowed to make her Communion long before the usual time permitted. The account of her First Communion is one of the most beautiful things in her life. "I felt that I was loved," she says, "and I said to Jesus: 'I love You and I give You myself for ever.'" Here is the beginning of that offering to the merciful Love of God, which was to be the mainspring of her prayer, and the source of her power over souls.

In Carmel her devotion to the Blessed Sacrament grew and deepened to a degree most rare in those days.

As a child she had made a rule never to ask her confessor to increase the number of Communions. In Carmel, however, she changed her mind. "I should set about it in a different way now," she wrote, "for I am convinced that one should tell one's director if one feels a longing to receive Our Lord. It is not in order to remain in a golden ciborium that He comes down from Heaven every day, but to find another Heaven; the Heaven of our soul, where He delights to dwell."

During and for a short time after the severe epidemic of influenza which swept through Carmel, she had the great joy of making her Communion daily, but this did not last for long. The Mother Prioress at the time was opposed to daily Communion as being an innovation. St Teresa said to her: "Mother, when I am dead I will make you change your mind." This prophecy she fulfilled. Five days after her death the new chaplain of Carmel urged the community to a daily Communion, and the Mother Prioress gave the Sisters permission to make their Communion every day.

In the Canonization process we read that at Carmel she appealed, in her ardent prayer and longings, for some word from the Pope to set souls free from all the rules and customs of communities which prevented daily Communion.

Her prayers and longings were also to be fulfilled, for, after her death, it was on reading the Saint's letters to her cousin, Marie, that Pope Pius X broke out into the exclamation: "Most opportune! Most opportune!" and gave orders for the process of Beatification to be begun at once.

It was Pius X who gave to the Church the decree urging daily Communion.

The Blessed Scrament absorbed her. At the end we see her struggling down to Mass when she was almost too weak to move, offering her fatigue for the missionaries abroad. Why was this? She tells us herself: "The Altar is a new Calvary where His Blood still flows for me."[1]

To her, the Blessed Sacrament was, above all, the Bread of the children. All little children need nourishment that their little bodies may grow. The Children of God need spiritual nourishment, in order that their spiritual life may grow. The Blessed Sacrament is their food.

Thus, the Blessed Sacrament alone enables us to live fully the life of a child of God, because through it we live by the Very Life of the Divine Son. "O Bread of exiles, Host Sacred and Divine, it is not I that live, my life comes all from Thee."[2]

Hence flow all the virtues of the Little Way, for He who first trod it lived in her. In giving her His Son to live in her, the Father had

[1] *Poem* "The Tabernacle."
[2] *Poem* "Remember."

indeed given her Himself. It is the Father stooping down to His child, taking her into His arms, and saying: "All that I have is thine." She is to live by His Life; she is to love with His Love. "Thy Love runs even to folly,"[1] she said, as she contemplated the mystery of the Host. She will do the same: "I have only one desire, to love Jesus unto folly." She is to be humble with His Humility: "O my Beloved, under the white eucharistic veil Thou dost indeed appear to me meek and humble of heart. To teach me humility Thou canst not further abase Thyself. So I wish to respond to Thy Love by often saying to Thee: 'Jesus, meek and humble of heart, make my heart like unto Thine.'"[2] She is to be confident with the Confidence with which the Divine Victim, her Saviour, committed Himself to His Father's Love in the darkness and desolation of Calvary. All His Abandonment is to belong to her, for, in possessing the Host within she possesses Him who died on Calvary serenely surrendered to His Father's will. She, too, would die serenely abandoned to her Heavenly Father's Love, with the words: "Father, into Thine Hands I commend my spirit," on her lips. Meditating on this, she cries: "How, then, can my confidence have any bounds?"[3]

All this we, too, possess, because we all possess the Host. We live by His Life, we love with His Love, we can be humble with His Humility, we can be confident with the Confidence of the Son of God. The source of sancity for us is the same as it was for her. Therefore, her prayer of the Little Way is possible for all of us.

This life of intimate union with her Lord through the Blessed Sacrament was not merely an emotional experience. As a result of Original Sin union with God on earth is always the way of the Cross, the way of faith in darkness and in suffering; we walk now by faith and not by sight. She had no visions. "There is no ecstasy," she says, "to which I do not prefer the monotony of hidden sacrifice."[4] Through the Blessed Sacrament we get back all that was lost. But in this land of exile

---

[1] A., p. 208.
[2] A., p. 453.
[3] A., p. 208.
[4] S., p. 27.

we must live by faith. In the Host is contained all that constitutes the Beatific Vision, yet to the outward eye we see only the appearance of bread. Here, focused to a point, we have all the asceticism of Catholic piety. We grasp the mystery of the Mass by faith; "the evidence of things that appear not"[1]; and thus, grasping God by faith, we grasp Him to the fullest degree possible on earth, in a supernatural manner which infinitely transcends any natural experience. It is this mortification of feeling, this homage of our intellect to faith, which keeps us humble, for we know it is none of our achieving. Thus it is that devotion to Our Lord in the Blessed Sacrament must always produce humility of heart, the childlike soul which rests in the Heavenly Father's embrace in abandonment and unquestioning love. In this union through faith is the love of the children for their Heavenly Father made perfect.

It was by union with the Divine Victim on the Cross, through the Mass, that St Teresa was able to offer herself so fully as a victim to the merciful Love, and, in return, it was in the Mass supremely that the Heavenly Father allowed the floods of infinite tenderness pent up in His Heart to overflow into her soul.

And so it is in the Postcommunion appointed for the Mass of the Saint that our Mother the Church puts upon the lips of all who would follow St Teresa as little victims of the merciful Love this beautiful prayer:—

"May the Heavenly Mystery, O Lord, inflame us with that fire of love wherewith the Virgin Saint Teresa offered herself to Thee as a victim of charity for all mankind. Through Our Lord Jesus Christ."

There is no other way by which Our Lord can fashion that legion of little victims to the merciful Love for which St Teresa so ardently pleaded when she was on this earth, and for which she appeals so powerfully now in Heaven.

Thus we see that the prayer of St Teresa all flows from the two words, "Our Father." It is the prayer of a little child to its Father. Therefore,

[1] Heb. xi. 1.

it is a prayer of loving dependence and complete confidence and abandonment, expressed always with absolute simplicity.

This prayer is possible to us all, because we all possess within our souls the identical source from which St Teresa drew all her power to pray. That source is the Holy Trinity dwelling within us—the Holy Trinity, whose very work it is to restore to us the supernatural Life of God which we had lost, and so to enable us once more to say "Our Father" in all its fullness, through a life of simple prayer, loving and humble, yet confident with the complete abandonment of a little child, serene in its father's arms.

And thus to console the Heart of Our Heavenly Father, to draw down His love more fully into our own hearts, and to win others to love Him, too.

Finally we have seen how all this is focused to a point in the Mass. The sacrifice of Our Blessed Lord is the one perfect prayer. Through Calvary and through Calvary alone we are reconciled to Our Father and restored to sonship. And so it comes to pass that in the Mass the first words which the priest says aloud, after the consecration, in the name of all the faithful, are "Our Father."

Here we are all lifted up into the perfect prayer of Our Lord Jesus Christ, here alone in the Mass through Him, with Him, and in Him can we pray with that love, dependence, and confidence which marks the prayer of all true children. Here alone can we say, with all their truest meaning, these two simple words, "Our Father."

THE PRAYER OF ST TERESA OF LISIEUX - PART II

Vernon Johnson

CONTENTS

PART II

V.   ST TERESA'S PRAYER IN PRACTICE

    In Consolation 37

    In Dryness.. 41

    In Suffering 44

VI. OUR LADY AND ST TERESA'S PRAYER 53

VII. THE PROVIDENTIAL MISSION OF ST TERESA'S PRAYER.......... 58

VIII. ST TERESA'S ACT OF OBLATION 60

The author wishes to express his deep gratitude to the Carmelites of Lisieux without whose supervision and encouragement this little book would never have been written.

In the chapter on "Dryness in Prayer" the author wishes to express his indebtedness to *The Science of Prayer* by Ludovic de Besse, O.S.F.C.

A.—Autobiography; L.—Laveille; N.V.—Novissima Verba; S.—Spirit of St Teresa.

PART II

THE PRAYER OF ST TERESA
IN PRACTICE

In Consolation

We have seen so far the characteristics of the prayer of St Teresa—namely, its love and humility, its confidence, abandon, and simplicity. We have seen also the place which the Mass held in her prayer. We will now see how this prayer worked out in her life.

That St Teresa had moments of consolation is clear from what she tells us in her Autobiography. The occasions, however, upon which she mentions them are but rare; and even of these few can be described as extraordinary consolations. For the most part they were ordinary, and she attached no great importance to them.

Of the occasions which she mentions during the years before she entered Carmel, the most striking are her miraculous cure by Our Lady and her first Communion.

Speaking of the former, she says: "The look upon Our Lady's face was inexpressibly kind and sweet, but what penetrated to the very depths of my soul was her gracious smile. Instantly all my pain vanished, my eyes filled, my tears fell silently, tears of purest heavenly joy."[1]

In describing her first Communion, she says: "My joy became so intense, so deep, that it could not be restrained: tears of happiness

---

[1] A., p. 66.

welled up and overflowed.... All the joy of Heaven had come down into one heart; and that heart—exiled, weak, and mortal—could not contain it without tears."[1]

At this early age of eleven we find a distinct blending of suffering with her joy. She speaks of her heart as "exiled, weak, and mortal." We notice it again in her account of her second Communion: "My tears flowed with inexpressible sweetness after my Communion.... I felt an urgent desire for suffering, as well as a conviction that I should have many a cross to bear. Then a wave of consolation flowed over my soul, such consolation as in all my life I have never known. Suffering became my treasure."[2] Thus, even the moment which she described as the moment of greatest consolation is again inseparably linked with suffering.

Still, the early days of the Saint were, generally speaking, days of consolation and of a conscious realization of God's Love. "Our Lord did indeed lavish His favours on His little flower.... And because I was small and frail He deigned to stoop down to me and instruct me gently in the secrets of His Love."[3]

After the Saint's entry into Carmel, she mentions only two occasions of extraordinary consolations and graces in prayer.

The first, which she experienced in the Convent garden in July, 1889, she described to her sister when she was dying: "It was as if a veil had been thrown over me, hiding all the things of earth.... I seemed to be entirely hidden beneath the veil of the Blessed Virgin. I had charge of the refectory, and I did things as if I did them not. It was as if I moved with a borrowed body. I remained like that for an entire week. It is a supernatural state very difficult to explain. God alone can put us into it, and it sometimes suffices to detach a soul for ever from the world."[4] Even this, it is to be noticed, she did not think important enough to mention in the Autobiography.

[1] A., p. 74.
[2] A., p. 76.
[3] A., p. 92.
[4] N.V., p. 56.

The second occasion she does mention in the Autobiography, but only in passing. She speaks of it as being the result of her Act of Oblation. "Dear Mother, you who allowed me to offer myself thus to God, you know the flames of love, or rather the oceans of grace, which filled my soul when I made that Act of Oblation on June 9th, 1895. Since that day Love surrounds and penetrates me; at every moment God's merciful Love renews and purifies me, cleansing my soul from all trace of sin."[1] This she described at length to her sister during her last illness: "I had commenced the Stations of the Cross in the choir, when, all at once, I felt myself wounded by a dart of fire so radiant that I thought I must die. I do not know how to explain it. It was as if an invisible hand had plunged me wholly into the fire. What fire! And what sweetness at the same time! I was burned with love, and I thought: 'One minute, nay, one second more, and I shall not be able to support such ardour without dying.' I understood then what the Saints have said of those states which they have experienced so often. For me, I have experienced it that once, only for an instant, and afterwards I fell back again into my habitual dryness."[2] In describing this special grace, she is careful to add that, unlike many of the Saints, she had experienced this but once, and that immediately it was succeeded by that dryness which was the normal state of her soul.

There is no doubt that she had moments of consolation at other times, as, for example, in the scene where she was found meditating on the words, "Our Father." At other moments we get glimpses of them, as when she says: "He only rarely allows me to see the effects of His Mercy…. Otherwise I could never survive the sweetness."[3] It would be unnatural if it were not so, and would be contrary to the way in which the Heavenly Father has always led His children.

The reason why she mentions these moments of consolation so rarely is because she knew that holiness, union with her Heavenly Father, did not consist in such consolations. That was not her

[1] A., p. 148.
[2] N.V., p. 44.
[3] A., p. 225.

39

Little Way. Her union with God, intimate as it was, was simply the development of the life of sanctifying grace, the Life of the Holy Trinity, planted in her soul at Baptism, and developed in her through a life of eucharistic love based, not on feeling, but on faith. Writing to Céline, she says: "If He lead us to Mount Tabor, it is but for one brief moment."[1] And, in a letter to Mother Agnes, we read: "I know of no ecstasy to which I do not prefer sacrifice. There I find happiness, and there alone."[2]

The reason is not far to seek. It is because the sole object of her prayer was to love Our Lord for His own sake, and so to console the Heart of the Heavenly Father, not by a life which should be selfishly dependent on consolation, but by a life which should be purified from every selfish motive, a life which lives by faith, loving God for His own sake alone.

We all possess these same means of holiness, because we all possess the Holy Trinity within us. This gift is nourished in all of us by our holy Mother the Church, through the Blessed Sacrament, so that the life of each one of us can be a life of eucharistic love, made perfect, not by feeling and consolation, but through simple faith in the promises of Our Lord and the Sacraments of His Church.

This is the simple Catholic way, by which we can, one and all, grow in love for Our Blessed Lord. Thus we can learn to console the Heart of Our Heavenly Father by a life of prayer, not nourished upon consolation, but purified from every selfish motive by the life of faith, by which we shall love Him for His own sake, and for His own sake alone.

This life of simple and loving prayer, based upon faith and not on feeling, is the answer to the subjective, restless, dissatisfied outlook of the world. Here again we see St Teresa as our God-given guide.

---

[1] A., p. 345.
[2] A., p. 352.

In Dryness

From the moment of her entry into Carmel, the way chosen by her Heavenly Father for St Teresa, so far from being a way of consolation, was instead a way of continual darkness and dryness.

"From the very outset," she tells us, "my soul had for its daily nourishment nothing but bitter dryness."[1] The passages in which she describes this spiritual dryness are among the most beautiful in her story, and full of the most precious teaching for those who would follow her Little Way. She shows us the reason for this dryness, the spirit in which to receive it, and what we should do when these times of dryness come.

One of these passages is a description of the retreat before her clothing, when we should have expected her to have received special consolation. "Dryness and drowsiness—such is the state of my soul in its intercourse with Jesus. How kind He is, this God who will soon be my Spouse. He is divinely lovable for not permitting me to be the captive of any passing joy. He knows well that if He sent me but a shadow of earthly happiness, I should cling to it with all the intense ardour of my heart, and so He refuses even this shadow. He prefers to leave me in darkness, rather than afford me a false glimmer which would not be Himself. All, all shall be for Him! And even when I have nothing, as is the case to-night, I will give Him this nothing."[2]

Could any words be more telling? We see the reality of the dryness, the sensitiveness of her soul, which might so easily be drawn away from her love of Jesus by a false consolation; her realization that that is why her Heavenly Father does not let her have it; her gratitude for the darkness, which she sees is His Love drawing her to Him alone in an act of perfect love; lastly the complete response of her ardent soul: "All, all shall be for Him." And so she falls asleep with the confidence and abandon of a little child, where others would lie awake and fret.

[1] A., p. 122.
[2] A., p. 352.

It is vital that those who are to follow the Little Way of St Teresa should understand what was happening here. We see her mind utterly powerless to devote itself to things divine, or to have an experience of them: her heart is absolutely dry; far from experiencing sweet, delightful emotions which attract it towards God, it only feels aversion and disgust. On the other hand, her will is strongly directed towards God; it feels the need of Him, and it has no peace except in clinging to Him. "All, all shall be for Him."

But this is not the whole story. It is not a mere clinging on in the dark, a purely negative prayer. This prayer of faith, she tells us so herself, definitely enriched her soul with a knowledge of God—God being infinitely above anything which she could either understand or feel. She just abandoned herself to Him in the darkness of a general faith, in order to arrive at a deeper knowledge of Him.

How did her Heavenly Father give her this knowledge of Himself? Without sound of words, without the intervention of any bodily or spiritual sense, as it were in silence and repose, in the darkness of sense and nature, He taught her soul, she knew not how, in a most secret and hidden way.

"The Teacher of teachers instructs without sound of words, and though I have never heard Him speak, yet I know He is within me, always guiding and inspiring me—and just when I need Him, light hitherto unseen breaks in upon me—as a rule it is not during prayer that this happens, but in the midst of my daily duties."[1]

We shall now see how perfectly this prayer works out in the ordinary details of life. For, in this kind of prayer, St Teresa did not form any particular desires, in fact we know she carefully avoided this; but her soul was content with a general desire to be united to her Heavenly Father by a loving obedience to everything He wished. She merely said "Our Father" in simplicity and abandonment. She desired to prove the sincerity of her love by obeying her Heavenly Father in everything; the details of this obedience did not concern her at all. She knew that her

---

[1] A., p. 147.

Heavenly Father would arrange all this, and that it would come to her from the commands of her superiors, from the ordinary duties of the day, and the ordinary contacts with the souls amongst whom she lived. Thus her prayer was vitally interwoven with all the details of every day. A perfect harmony existed between activity and abandonment in her prayer. "Thérèse is far from the heights of fervour at this moment, but when I am in this state of spiritual dryness, unable to pray, or even to practise virtue, I look for little opportunities, for the smallest trifles, to please Jesus; a smile or a kind word for instance, when I would wish to be silent or to show that I am bored. If no such occasions offer, I try at least to say over and over again that I love Him. This is not hard, and it keeps alive the fire in my heart. Even should the fire of love seem dead, I would still throw my tiny straws on the ashes, and I am confident it would light up again. It is true I am not always faithful, but I never lose courage. I leave myself in the arms of Our Lord."[1]

What priceless lessons are contained in these words! A Saint who cannot pray, a Saint who cannot practise virtue! What an encouragement this should be for us! Now notice the simplicity of her solution; just little acts of love, just the most ordinary things of everyday life, a word or a smile. And so her life of activity is closely interwoven with her prayer. Should these little acts of love fail, or occasions not present themselves of doing them, she simply tells Our Lord again and again that she loves Him. Sometimes it is hard, sometimes love seems dead, and sometimes she fails even here. But, in the complete confidence of a little child, she goes on, leaving herself in the arms of Our Lord, a perfect blend of the passive and the active, activity within perfect rest, a foretaste upon earth of the life of Heaven.

In her retreat before Profession (September, 1890) she experienced the same dryness. "Far from receiving consolation, I went through the retreat in a state of utter dryness and as if abandoned by God; instead of being grieved, I am glad."[2] Such was her experience at moments of

---

[1] A., p. 345.
[2] A., p. 134.

her life when we should have expected that she would be most consoled. But, indeed, it was her normal state. We have seen how she meets it. She is not idle, nor is her abandonment an inactive acceptance of the Divine plan. "Sometimes, when I am in such a state of spiritual dryness that not a single good thought occurs to me, I say very slowly the 'Our Father' or the 'Hail, Mary,' and these prayers suffice to take me out of myself and wonderfully refresh me."[1] A remedy so simple that we have probably never thought of it. The danger of spiritual dryness is that it turns us in upon ourselves in self-pity. She does the exact opposite. She says the "Our Father" and "Hail, Mary" very slowly. At once the whole family of her Father fills her mind—Our Lady, the Annunciation, sinners, the hour of our death. So she forgets her dryness. And so shall we. But we must be very little children of Our Heavenly Father to pray with such simplicity as this.

In Suffering

We have seen how Our Blessed Lord, from the very beginning, led St Teresa in her prayer by the path, not of feeling, but of faith; giving her, as she said, dryness and darkness, in order that, in her prayer, she might give Him a love free from all self-interest, a love which should love Him for Himself alone.

We are now going to see how Our Blessed Lord finally perfected the prayer of St Teresa till it became an act of perfect love, secure in its humility, radiant in its confidence, serene in its abandon and its simplicity. We shall see how, in so doing, He drew forth such a complete surrender to the workings of His merciful Love in her soul that at last, stripped of self, she was able, by her love, to offer to Him that consolation which she had so longed to give Him, and through her sacrifice and suffering, was able to be a perfect instrument for winning other souls to love Him, too; thus again consoling the longing of her Heavenly Father's Heart.

---

[1] A., p. 180.

When Our Lord was on this earth, it was the Cross which was the perfect expression of His Love for the Father and of the Father's Love for Him: "Therefore doth the Father love me because I lay down my life."[1] And again: "That the world may know that I love the Father, even so I do."[2] And He went straight to His Cross. It was by the Cross, at the same time, that Our Lord won back for the Father the love of the children who had rejected Him. In other words, the means He chose were suffering, physical and spiritual, and finally death, that through this Death they might have life everlasting.

"It is sufficient for the disciple that he be as his master." Thus we find that He gives the same to all His Saints. And so He gives to St Teresa suffering, physical and spiritual, bodily pain and spiritual desolation. And this was exactly what her ardent soul desired, for did she not say herself: "The death of love which I desire is the Death of Jesus on the Cross."[3]

Physical Suffering

Two years before her death St Teresa developed consumption, and consumption of a very painful kind. The disease steadily sapped her bodily strength. She met it with joy. The doctor attending her could not understand it. "If only you knew what this young nun is suffering," he said; "never have I seen such suffering borne with such supernatural joy." Her sufferings were intense "Oh, my Mother, what does it signify to write eloquently about suffering? Nothing! Nothing! One must be in it."[4]

What supports her in this moment of utter weakness? It is her dependence upon her Heavenly Father. She looks to Him with the helplessness of a little child. "Oh, my Mother, what would become of me if God did not give me His strength? I have only my hands free. One would never believe it possible to suffer like this. No, it must be

[1] John x. 17.
[2] John xiv. 31.
[3] A., p. 240.
[4] N.V., p. 180.

45

experienced to be understood."[1] Only her hands free—the helplessness of it! But it is this very helplessness which flings her into her Heavenly Father's arms. "I have passed such a bad night. How good God is in enabling me to bear all I suffer. Even yet I do not believe I am at the end of suffering, but He will never abandon me."[2]

What was the sort of prayer that St Teresa said in this great trial? It was the simplest possible. She was reduced to such physical weakness that she could hardly move. "What courage I need," she says, "to make even the sign of the Cross. 'My God, my God, have mercy upon me.' That is all I can say."[3]

In consequence of her extreme weakness she almost fainted on the occasion of her last Communion. "Oh," she said, "if only one knew what this trial is like. This night, being unable to do more, I have just asked the Blessed Virgin to take my head in her hands, so that I might be able to bear it."[4] Her devotion to Our Lady during these days of suffering was very beautiful. "Pray much to the Blessed Virgin for me," she said; "if you were sick I should pray much for you."[5] When all connected and continuous prayers became quite impossible, her childlike simplicity was never at a loss, and we get this exquisite incident. Being in great pain, she told one of her sisters this: "I can only look at Our Blessed Lady and say, 'Jesus.'"[6] What prayer could be more powerful with Our Holy Mother than a glance at her and the mention of the Holy Child? Could any prayer be a more perfect expression of the Little Way of Spiritual Childhood? Its absolute simplicity, its unquestioning confidence, its utter spontaneity; through it all her love and confidence shine out radiant. "Is it hard to suffer so much?" they asked her.

"No," she replied, "I am still able to tell God that I love Him, and that is enough." Later on she was unable even to do this. All words

[1] N.V., p. 146.
[2] N.V., p. 147.
[3] N.V., p. 164.
[4] N.V., p. 139.
[5] N.V., p. 148.
[6] N.V., p. 206.

became impossible. The infirmarian found her late one night with her hands joined and her eyes raised towards Heaven.

"What are you doing?" she asked; "you ought to try to get some sleep."

"I cannot, Sister," the Saint replied; "I am suffering too much, so I pray."

"What do you say to Jesus?" the Sister asked her.

"I say nothing. I just love Him."[1]

She loved Him in it and through it all, because she saw that her suffering was just His merciful Love drawing her into closer union with Him. Far from praying to escape from suffering, she prays with complete abandonment that nothing may hinder this work of Love. Someone said to her: "I pray that you may not suffer so much, and you suffer still more."

"And I," replied St Teresa, "have asked God not to hear the prayers which would place an obstacle to the accomplishment of His plan for me."[2]

Finally, unable to say her Office, unable to meditate, unable to use her rosary, unable even to think of God or prayer, she says this lovely thing: "'What is my spiritual life in sickness?' you ask me. It is to suffer, and that is all."[3]

Instead of giving in and saying that there was nothing that she could do, that all spiritual life was made impossible for her by her pain and her disease, instead of being disheartened and depressed, with her simple and confident love she seizes on the one thing left and makes it her all. She joyously surrenders herself to her consumption; her consumption becomes her spiritual life, her consumption becomes her prayer, becomes the expression of her love, becomes her Little Way to the Heart of the Heavenly Father and to the heart of all humanity, for whom, in joyous silence, she offers up all her pain.

---

[1] A., p. 237.
[2] N.V., p. 129.
[3] N.V., p. 108.

Worn out by physical suffering, St Teresa was unable at times, as we have seen, to pray either by word or thought, so that her suffering became her only prayer. Along with this physical suffering there went an even more penetrating trial. Her Heavenly Father allowed her, His little child, to suffer from continual and terrible temptations against the Faith. It was some eighteen months before her death that these temptations against the Faith began. She thus describes these attacks of the devil. "You dream," he says, mockingly, "of a land of light and fragrance, you believe that the Creator of these wonders will be for ever yours, you think to escape one day from the mists in which you now languish. Hope on! Hope on! Look forward to death! It will give you not what you hope for, but a night darker still, the night of utter nothingness."[1] How does she meet it? By prayer. And her prayer took the form of acts of faith of the simplest possible kind, with which she holds at bay these terrible temptations. "May God forgive me! He knows how I try to live by faith, even though it affords me no consolation. I have made more acts of faith during the past year than in all the rest of my life."[2] She goes further. With a little child's genius for love she makes it an opportunity of deepening her love for her Heavenly Father. So she replies to these attacks by simply increasing her acts of love. "Hastening to my Saviour, I tell Him that I am ready to shed my blood as a witness to my belief in Heaven."[3] Not only this, but her temptation becomes a means whereby her insatiable love for souls shall find expression, and she offers her darkness for the conversion of unbelievers: "I tell Jesus that if He will deign to open it for eternity to poor unbelievers, I am content to sacrifice during my life all joyous thoughts of the Home that awaits me." And again: "In spite of this trial which robs me of all sense of enjoyment, I can still say: 'Thou hast

---

[1] A., p. 157.
[2] A., p. 157.
[3] A., p. 157.

given me, O Lord, a delight in Thy doings.' For is there a greater joy than to suffer for Thy Love, O my God?"[1]

In her last illness all this was deepened and intensified. It was especially in her prayer that the devil was allowed to attack her. "Pray for me," she says, "for often when I cry to Heaven for help, it is then that I feel most abandoned."[2]

Some time before she had written these words: "It has pleased Almighty God to reveal to me that the only way to perfection is the way of the little child who sleeps without fear in its father's arms."[3] It is exactly that abandonment, without reserve, into her Father's arms which makes possible the height of sanctity which we now are witnessing. In earlier days she used to desire suffering and death. Now all that is over. She desires now nothing except the fulfilment of the Father's Will. "Love alone draws me. I wish for neither suffering nor death, yet both are precious to me. I have long called upon them as the messengers of joy, but now the spirit of self-abandonment is my sole guide. I have no other compass. I am no longer eager for anything except the accomplishment of God's design for my soul."[4]

So trusting not in herself, but in the power of sanctifying grace, living and loving with the Life and Love of the Holy Trinity within her, she moves along the path to her perfection, turning her trial into joy, using it to make that act of perfect love with which she would console her Heavenly Father's Heart and with which she would win other souls to love her Heavenly Father, too.

On the night of August 6th it seemed impossible that she should live. In the morning she said: "I have awaited Jesus all the night. I have resisted many temptations. Oh, how many acts of faith I have made."[5] Her childlike spirit was invincible. She turns every trial into love.

"Apparently the Saints have forsaken you," said a Sister.

[1] A., p. 157.
[2] A., p. 222.
[3] A., p. 197.
[4] A., p. 146.
[5] N.V., p. 113.

She replied: "I love them very much all the same. They only want to see how far I can push my confidence."[1] She loved the Saints for seeming to abandon her, because she saw that it was all part of the Family affair by which the Heavenly Father and His children in Heaven were drawing the little one on earth to live by faith. "I often pray to the Saints without being heard, but the more deaf they appear to be the more I love them. I do not desire to see either God or the Saints, but to rest in this dark night of faith. Let others desire to see all and understand all."[2]

All the characteristics of her prayer shone out especially on her last day on earth. Desolation, love, surrender, confidence, all are focused to a point in the last few words that she uttered. In the early morning, while the others were at Mass, she said: "Oh how fervently I have prayed to Our Lady, but it is all pure agony, without one ray of consolation."[3] Her confidence and abandonment remained unshaken. "God is not going to abandon me. He has never abandoned me yet. Yes, my God, do all You will, but have mercy upon me. My God, You are so good."

The Blessed Virgin is ever with her. "Oh, my Mother," she says to the Prioress, "present me very soon to the Blessed Virgin. Prepare me to die well." The Prioress replied that she was fully prepared, because she was so humble. "Yes, it seems to me that I have never sought anything but the truth. Yes, I have understood humility of heart." Never for a moment does she falter in the confidence with which she offers herself through suffering to the working of the Love of her merciful Father in her soul. "All that I have written about my desire for suffering, Oh yes, it is quite true. I do not repent of having delivered myself up to Love. Quite the contrary." Twice she repeated these words. From the surrender of herself as a victim of her Heavenly Father's Love, she passes to the offering of her pain for the winning of souls to that Love. "I would never have believed it possible to suffer so much, never, never.

[1] N.V., p. 177.
[2] N.V., p. 131.
[3] N.V., pp. 193-195.

I can only explain it by the ardent desire I have to save souls." Thus the offering of herself in an act of perfect love to the merciful Love of God is not for one moment separated from the offering of herself for the souls of men. Her sufferings reach out to the furthest missions of the Church. A little later, in great anguish: "I cannot breathe, I cannot die, but I am very willing to suffer more." To die of love had always been the goal of her heart. That goal is drawing near now. "All my smallest desires," she murmured, "have been realized, and the greatest of all, to die of love, must be realized, too."

At seven o'clock in the evening she turned to the Prioress and said: "Mother, is it not yet the agony? Am I not yet going to die?" On the Mother Prioress telling her that the agony would probably be prolonged, she replied: "Ah well, so be it, so be it. I do not wish to suffer less." With this act of complete resignation on her lips, she turned towards her Crucifix and said very slowly: "Oh!...I love Him!...My God...I...love...Thee."[1]

She then fell back upon her pillow, and all seemed over. When suddenly she raised herself, and opening her eyes, which shone with a happiness surpassing all her hopes, she fixed her gaze a little above the statue of Our Lady. She remained there for the space of a Credo, and then she gave up her soul to her Heavenly Father, to the last His little child.

So St Teresa died,[2] and her last words on earth were an act of love made in the dark of physical suffering and spiritual desolation. Thus was fulfilled her desire to die as her Lord had died, the death of love upon the Cross.

Thus did her Heavenly Father purify the soul of His little child in the furnace of His Love.

Along the road of Calvary, which He first had trod, Our Lord led her through suffering, physical and spiritual, to that perfect union with

---

[1] A., p. 240.
[2] Sept. 30th, 1897.

Him for which she longed. In the darkness, walking by faith, she was able to make that act of perfect love which she so desired, by which she could console her Father and which she could offer for the souls of men. This work is now made perfect. Nothing of Self remains. She offered herself to the Divine merciful Love. This merciful Love has now consumed her, purifying her from all Self, so that she has become one act of love. Her soul, now ready, bursts the bonds of her mortal body and finds its home in her Father's arms.

The work of sanctifying grace is done. Through correspondence with the Holy Trinity within her, her life has become one act of supernatural love, inspired and directed by the Holy Spirit of Love Himself. Thus she becomes, to the fullest degree possible for her in the Divine Plan, a partaker in the Divine Nature, a perfect child of her Heavenly Father. Her whole being says just two words, "Our Father." As she dies to this world she becomes a living Paternoster.

OUR LADY AND THE PRAYER OF ST TERESA

No treatise on the prayer of St Teresa would be complete which did not mention Our Lady.

"Oh, how I love Our Blessed Mother.... She is more Mother than Queen!"[1] These words of St Teresa tell us the place which Our Lady holds in the Little Way of Spiritual Childhood, and therefore in the prayer of St Teresa. As she trod the Little Way she always looked upon Our Blessed Mother with the eyes of a little child, and so it is her Motherhood which captivated St Teresa's heart. In her meditation on the Gospel she sees Our Blessed Lord perform His first public miracle at the request of His Blessed Mother, and at once Our Lady becomes for her her Mother tenderly interested in all her children and interceding for them in all their needs. Thus to St Teresa Our Lady was the Mother of divine Grace because she was the Mother of Our Blessed Lord from whom all grace flows, and also because it was her special privilege to bestow all grace upon her children in answer to their prayer. "When we pray to the Saints they make us wait a little. One feels that they have to go and present their requests to Our Lord. But when I ask for a grace from the Blessed Virgin the help I receive is immediate."[2]

Before writing the Autobiography, now loved throughout the world, she commended it to Our Lady. "Before setting about my task I knelt before the statue of Our Lady which had given my family so many proofs of Our Heavenly Mother's loving care. As I knelt, I begged of

[1] N.V., p. 152.
[2] Summarium.

that dear Mother to guide my hand and thus ensure that only what was pleasing to her should find place here."[1]

In describing her first confession she says: "I remember well how the priest exhorted me above all to a tender devotion towards Our Lady, and I promised to redouble my love for her who already filled so large a place in my heart."[2]

In her grave illness it was to her Mother she turned for help, and it was by her Mother that she was cured. "Utterly exhausted with pain I turned to my Heavenly Mother, begging her from the bottom of my heart to have pity on me…then all my pain vanished."[3] St Teresa was completely cured.

It was to Mary, the Mother of Divine Grace, that she made her act of consecration on the day of her first communion. "With all my heart I consecrated myself to the Blessed Virgin Mary and asked her to watch over me…. Had she not herself on that morning of the 8th of May placed in the garden of my soul her son Jesus, the flower of the field and the lily of the valleys?"[4]

This complete dependence upon Our Blessed Mother continued during her life in Carmel. "I never reprimand you," she said to the novices, "without first invoking Our Blessed Lady and asking her to inspire me as to what will be for your good."

Towards the end we shall see her turning more and more to that Blessed Mother as the hour of her supreme trial draws near. In the last poem which she wrote as death was approaching we find these beautiful words:

"O thou who camest to smile on me at the dawn of life's beginning, Come, Mother, once again and smile for its drawing to eventide."

Her last morning on earth she said: "I have prayed all night to Our Lady; it was pure agony without a ray of consolation."

[1] A., p. 49.
[2] A., p. 49.
[3] A., p. 66.
[4] A., p. 75.

A little later she said to the Mother Prioress: "Present me to Our Lady. Prepare me to die well."

As the Convent bell rang the evening angelus she gazed with inexpressible tenderness upon the statue of the Immaculate Mother, and in her dying ecstasy it was just above the statue of Our Lady that her eyes were fixed.

To St Teresa, Our Blessed Lady, after her Divine Son, was the most perfect example of the Little Way. Bethlehem was the cradle of the Little Way and Nazareth the scene where it first was lived. So to the Mother of Bethlehem and Nazareth she turns for the graces necessary for her Little Way of Spiritual Childhood.

> "All that the Mother possesses belongs to her children, And I am thy child. O, my most cherished Mother, Thy virtue and thy love, do they not all belong to me?"

To St Teresa Our Lady's Little Way was the way of love, the way of Mary and Jesus was the way of a mother and her little one—all love! It was the way of simple humility. St Luke's account of the Annunciation fascinated her. The humility of Mary hidden in the silence of the Galilean hills—"He hath regarded the humility of His handmaiden!" It was the way of confidence and complete abandonment. At the very start, when even St Joseph was minded to put her away, she said nothing, but trusted solely in Heaven for her aid.

Through the flight into Egypt she remains unmoved, calmly she faces the approaching Passion till finally she stands at the foot of the Cross, a perfect example, from Bethlehem to Calvary, of the confidence and complete abandonment of the Little Way.

But, above all, Our Lady was to St Teresa the model of the Little Way of Spiritual Childhood because she was, after her Divine Son, the most perfect victim to the merciful Love of God.

From the first *fiat mihi* of the Annunciation through all the simple hidden routine of the life of Nazareth she offered herself day by day without any reserve to the workings of the merciful Love; through all the misunderstandings and hatred which closed in upon her Divine Son she offers herself unresisting, until she stands at the foot of the Cross a victim with the Divine Victim. The spear which pierced the Sacred Heart of her Son was indeed the sword which Simeon prophesied should pierce her own heart.

In giving her Son to the Cross she gave Him to be Our Saviour. At the foot of the Cross she stands as co-redemptrix with her Son in the supreme work of the merciful Love of God, the salvation of the human race. St Teresa loved to meditate upon the fact that it was at that very moment that Our Lord gave her to us as Our Mother—the Mother of the mystical body.

"He saith to His Mother; Woman, behold thy Son. After that, He saith to the disciple: Behold thy Mother."[1]

Her sufferings on Calvary were indeed the birthpangs by which Our Mother brought us her children forth to supernatural life. On Calvary Our Lord gives her to us as our spiritual Mother.

To St Teresa, her Mother, as she stood at the foot of the Cross, was indeed the Mother of Consolation, consoling the heart of the Heavenly Father by her perfect surrender to the workings of His love, and so drawing down that love in fullest measure into her soul. At that moment she became the Mother of Consolation for all her children too, because by that very surrender she was drawing countless other souls to love their Heavenly Father also, and to find that peace which nothing else can give.

So St Teresa turns to her Heavenly Mother to help her in her desire to be a victim of the merciful Love, to offer herself in every detail of her life, so that, emptied of all self, the Divine Love might flood her and possess her soul. With her Mother she would stand at the foot of the Cross to console Our Lord for His rejection by men; like her she would become a Mother of souls by catching the precious blood and pouring

---

[1] John xix. 26.

it out upon souls by her life of prayer and sacrifice. So her Mother, Mary, was "little Teresa's" constant companion as she trod her Little Way through the simple details of her life in Carmel.

Thus St Teresa points us to Our Blessed Mother as our Companion and support as we tread the Little Way which Our Blessed Mother trod before us. Specially does St Teresa bid us turn to her at the last moment of our pilgrimage, when the devil will let loose all his assaults upon us.

At that moment, just as she stood by her dying Son, so she will stand by us, her little children; Mother of Divine Grace! Mother of Sorrows! Mother of Consolation! "Holy Mary, Mother of God; pray for us sinners now and at the hour of our death."

THE PROVIDENTIAL MISSION OF
ST TERESA'S PRAYER

"I beseech thee to cast Thy glance upon a vast number of little souls: I entreat Thee to choose in this world a legion of little victims worthy of Thy Love."

With this prayer St Teresa closes her Autobiography. She passes from human sight and enters Heaven. From that moment Almighty God has made known her Mission to the world with a rapidity and to an extent almost unparalleled in the history of the Church. What is this Mission? It is simply the fulfilment of this prayer. And the means which God has chosen by which that prayer should be fulfilled is the Saint herself.

Ever since she entered Heaven she has, through her Little Way of Spiritual Childhood, been drawing to Our Lord a vast number of little souls, a legion of little victims worthy of His Love. How? By teaching souls throughout the world to pray to God as little children to their Heavenly Father. For the prayer of the Little Way is the key to the life of the Little Way.

The religious houses of the Church in every part of the world are constantly opening their doors to souls drawn by the Saint and her simple way of prayer. In our own country the rapid development of Carmel followed close upon her death. Priests at home and in the Mission field bear witness in countless numbers to the fact that they owe their vocation to her, and that the permanent inspiration of their Priesthood is the Little Way of Spiritual Childhood and the simplicity of St Teresa's prayer. And thus down the years she multiplies the Mass, the one perfect and all sufficient prayer.

There is no section of the faithful which she does not touch. Those who are already devout she calls to yet deeper and ever simpler prayer, the careless, whom nothing else seems able to touch, are arrested by her attractive simplicity, and find themselves in prayer at the Sacred Feet. Those who are weary are refreshed by the buoyant spontaneity of her love. Complex and sophisticated souls, irritated at first, are won by her extreme simplicity. Out and out sinners, attracted by their opposite, fall captive to the purity of her love.

And one and all end by learning from her to pray as little children to their Father.

It was this which made Pope Pius XI end his homily of the Canonization with these words:—

"If the way of Spiritual Childhood became general, who does not see how easily would be realized the reformation of human society, which We set ourselves to accomplish at the commencement of Our Pontificate?…We therefore adopt as Ours the prayer of the new St Teresa with which she ends her invaluable Autobiography:—

"O Jesus, we beseech Thee to cast Thy glance upon a vast number of little souls and to choose in this world a legion of little victims worthy of Thy love. Amen."

OFFERING OF ST TERESA OF THE CHILD JESUS AS VICTIM OF HOLOCAUST TO THE MERCIFUL LOVE OF GOD

"O my God, most Blessed Trinity, I desire to love Thee and to make Thee loved, to labour for the glory of Holy Church by saving souls on earth and by delivering those who suffer in Purgatory. I desire to accomplish Thy Will perfectly and to attain to the degree of glory which Thou hast prepared for me in Thy Kingdom; in a word, I long to be a saint, but I know that I am powerless, and I implore Thee, O my God, to be Thyself my sanctity.

"Since Thou hast so loved me as to give me Thine only Son to be my Saviour and my Spouse, the infinite treasures of His merits are mine; to Thee I offer them with joy, beseeching Thee to behold me only through the eyes of Jesus and in His Heart burning with love.

"Again, I offer Thee all the merits of the saints in heaven and on earth, their acts of love and those of the holy angels. Lastly I offer Thee, O Blessed Trinity, the love and the merits of the Blessed Virgin, my most dear Mother; to her I entrust my oblation, begging her to present it to Thee. Her Divine Son, my well-beloved Spouse, during the days of His life on earth, told us 'If you ask the Father anything in My Name, He will give it to you.' I am then certain that Thou wilt hearken to my desires…My God, I know it, *the more Thou willest to give, the more dost Thou make us desire*. Immense are the desires that I feel within my heart and with confidence I call upon Thee to come and take possession of my soul. I cannot receive Thee in Holy Communion as often as I would, but, Lord, art Thou not Almighty?…Remain in me as in the Tabernacle, never leave Thy little victim….

"I long to console Thee for the ingratitude of the wicked, and I pray Thee to take from me the power to displease Thee. If through frailty I sometimes fall, may Thy Divine glance purify my soul immediately, consuming every imperfection, as fire transforms all things into itself.

"I thank Thee, O my God, for all the graces Thou hast showered on me, in particular for having made me pass through the crucible of suffering. With joy shall I behold Thee on the last day bearing Thy sceptre, the Cross. Since Thou hast deigned to give me for my portion this most precious Cross, I hope I may resemble Thee in heaven and see the sacred stigmata of Thy Passion shine on my glorified body.

"After this exile on earth, I hope to enjoy possession of Thee in the eternal Fatherland, but I have no wish to amass merits for heaven, I will work for Thy love alone, my sole aim being to give Thee pleasure, to console Thy Sacred Heart and to save souls who will love Thee for ever.

"At the close of this life I shall appear before Thee with empty hands, for I ask not, Lord, that Thou wouldst count my works…. All our good deeds are stained in Thy sight. I desire therefore to be clothed with Thine own Justice, and to receive from Thy *Love* the eternal possession of Thyself. I crave no other throne, no other crown but Thee, O my Beloved.

"In Thy sight, time is nothing; one day is as a thousand years. Thou canst in an instant prepare me to appear before Thee.

(The Indulgenced part)   (300 days of Indulgence)

"That my life may be one act of perfect love, *I offer myself as Victim of Holocaust to Thy merciful Love*, imploring Thee to consume me unceasingly, and to let the floodtide of infinite tenderness pent up in Thee, flow into my soul, that so I may become a martyr of Thy Love, O my God.

"May this martyrdom, after having prepared me to appear before Thee, break life's web at last, and may my soul take its flight, unhindered, to the eternal embrace of Thy *merciful Love*.

"I desire, O my Beloved, at every heartbeat to renew this oblation an infinite number of times, till the shadows fade away and I can tell Thee my love eternally face to face...."

(Signed) Marie-Françoise-Thérèse de l'Enfant Jésus et de la Sainte Face

(rel. carm. ind.)

Feast of the Most Holy Trinity, the 9th of June, in the year of Grace, 1895.